PENGUIN PAIRS: COUNTING BY 2s

by Amanda Doering Tourville

illustrated by Sharon Holm

Content Consultants: Paula J. Maida, PhD, and Terry Sinko, Instructional Support Teacher

magic wagon

VISIT US AT
WWW.ABDOPUBLISHING.COM

Published by Magic Wagon, a division of the ABDO Publishing Group, 8000 West 78th Street, Edina, Minnesota, 55439. Copyright © 2009 by Abdo Consulting Group, Inc. International copyrights reserved in all countries. All rights reserved. No part of this book may be reproduced in any form without written permission from the publisher.

Looking Glass Library™ is a trademark and logo of Magic Wagon.

Printed in the United States.

Text by Amanda Doering Tourville
Illustrations by Sharon Holm
Edited by Patricia Stockland
Interior layout and design by Becky Daum
Cover design by Becky Daum

Library of Congress Cataloging-in-Publication Data

Tourville, Amanda Doering, 1980–
 Penguin pairs : counting by 2s / by Amanda Doering Tourville ; illustrated by Sharon Holm.
   p. cm. — (Count the critters)
  ISBN 978-1-60270-265-3
 1. Counting—Juvenile literature. 2. Multiplication—Juvenile literature. 3. Penguins—Juvenile literature. I. Holm, Sharon Lane, ill. II. Title.
  QA113.T6865 2009
  513.2'11—dc22

2008001619

You can count faster when counting
by twos. Count by twos as these
Emperor penguins swim in the icy
cold waters near the South Pole.

Two penguins dive into the water.

They glide through the water with ease.

This pair of two penguins swims in the

icy cold water.

14 15 **16** 17 **18** 19 **20**   0+2=

Two more penguins dive into the water. They leave a trail of bubbles floating up behind them. Count them slowly: one, two, three, four.

Count them quickly in pairs: two, four. Four penguins swim in the icy cold water.

2+2=4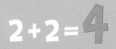

Two more penguins dive into the water. They press their feet close to their tails to steer. Count the pairs: two, four, six. Six penguins swim in the icy cold water.

14 15 16 17 18 19 20 4+2=6

Two more penguins dive into the water.
They flap their flippers to go faster.

Count the pairs: two, four, six, eight.

Eight penguins swim in the icy cold water.

14 15 **16** 17 **18** 19 **20**   6+2=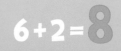

Two more penguins dive into the water.
They dart and dive after a school of fish.

Count the pairs: two, four, six, eight, ten. Ten penguins swim in the icy cold water.

14 15 **16** 17 **18** 19 **20**   8+2= 10

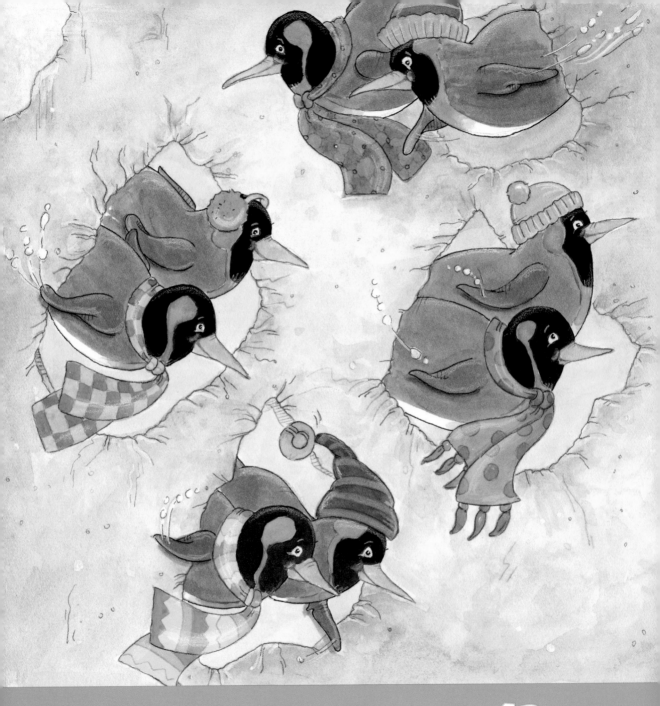

Two more penguins dive into
the water. They swim in and
out of caves made of ice.
Count the pairs: two, four, six,
eight, ten, twelve. Twelve penguins
swim in the icy cold water.

Two more penguins dive into the water.
They twist and turn to avoid a large
leopard seal. Count the pairs: two, four,
six, eight, ten, twelve, fourteen. Fourteen
penguins swim in the icy cold water.

14 15 **16** 17 **18** 19 **20**   12 + 2 = **14**

Two more penguins dive into the water. They circle and chase each other, playing a game. Count the pairs: two, four, six, eight, ten, twelve, fourteen, sixteen. Sixteen penguins swim in the icy cold water.

14 15 **16** 17 **18** 19 **20**   14+2= **16**

Two more penguins dive into the water. They swim close to the surface, diving in and out of the waves.

Count the pairs: two, four, six, eight, ten, twelve, fourteen, sixteen, eighteen. Eighteen penguins swim in the icy cold water.

Two more penguins dive into the water. They chase a slimy squid. Count the pairs: two, four, six, eight, ten, twelve, fourteen, sixteen, eighteen, twenty. Twenty penguins swim in the icy cold water.

Words to Know

flipper—a penguin's wings; penguins can not fly like other birds, but they have flippers to help them swim.

glide—to move smoothly.

icy—very cold.

steer—to guide and control the direction in which something moves.

Web Sites

To learn more about counting by 2s, visit ABDO Publishing Company on the World Wide Web at **www.abdopublishing.com**. Web sites about counting are featured on our Book Links page. These links are routinely monitored and updated to provide the most current information available.